MW01000087

Hot Glue
Hacks and Crafts

50 Fun and Creative Decor, Fashion,
Gift and Holiday Projects to Make
with Your Glue Gun

Angie Holden and Carolina Moore

Ulysses
Press

Text and photographs copyright © 2018 Angie Holden and Carolina Moore except as noted below. Design and concept copyright © 2018 Ulysses Press and its licensors. All rights reserved. Any unauthorized duplication in whole or in part or dissemination of this edition by any means (including but not limited to photocopying, electronic devices, digital versions, and the internet) will be prosecuted to the fullest extent of the law.

Published by Ulysses Press
P.O. Box 3440
Berkeley, CA 94703
www.ulyssespress.com

ISBN: 978-1-61243-833-7
Library of Congress Catalog Number 2018944072

Printed in Canada by Marquis Book Printing
10 9 8 7 6 5 4 3 2 1

Acquisitions editor: Casie Vogel
Managing editor: Claire Chun
Project editor: Claire Sielaff
Editor: Lauren Harrison
Proofreader: Shayna Keyles
Front cover and interior design and layout: what!design @ whatweb.com
Cover photographs: © Angie Holden and Carolina Moore
Interior photographs: © Angie Holden and Carolina Moore except Embellished Pillow (page 43)
   © Gina Luker; Fun Frames for Kids (page 45) © Kara Rodgerson; Floral Art Decor (page 46)
   © Jen Goode; Mason Jar Lid Wreath (page 48) © Jessica Hill; Stamped Fabric Pillow (page
   79) © Carissa Bonham; photo of Kara Rodgerson (page 127) © Shades of Green Multimedia;
   photos of Carissa Bonham (page 127) and authors (page 128) © Amanda Fomaro

Distributed by Publishers Group West

IMPORTANT NOTE TO READERS: This book is independently authored and published and no sponsorship or endorsement of this book by, and no affiliation with, any trademarked brands or products mentioned or pictured within is claimed or suggested. All trademarks that appear in this book belong to their respective owners and are used here for informational purposes only. The authors and publisher encourage readers to patronize the quality brands and products pictured and mentioned in this book.

To Randy, who puts up with my constant crafting. To Rebecca and Matthew, who are always willing to inspire me and lend a hand. To Elizabeth: without you, I wouldn't have a home for any of my wreaths. And to Cain: you keep me young. —Angie

To Jason, Logan, and Brandon, who inspire me every day. To my mom, who taught me to question limits. And to my dad, who gave me my love of books. —Carolina

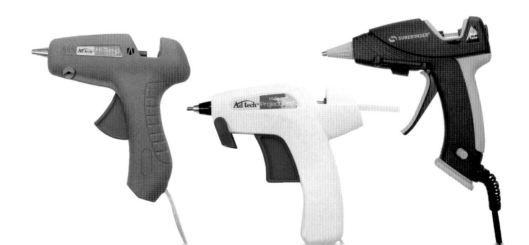

Contents

Hot Glue *Hacks and Crafts*

Introduction

You'll never look at a glue gun the same way again! From everyday uses to unbelievable hacks to "faux" creations made with hot glue, we've created the ultimate guide to stretching your glue gun to its limits.

Hot glue is a go-to for most crafters because it is inexpensive, easy to store, and easy to use. A quick dab of hot glue can be found in thousands of crafting projects. But this book uses much more than a few dabs! We wanted to go beyond even our own preconceptions of how hot glue could be used.

Any crafter will tell you that hot glue is a nearly ideal adhesive. It's simple to use, quick to dry, and creates a strong bond on most materials. But for this book, we didn't limit hot glue to the role of an adhesive—we made it the star of the show. Using colored glue or glitter glue, painting the glue, or letting the translucent glue stand alone, the projects in this book show you how a simple glue gun and a few sticks of glue can create wonders.

As professional crafters, we have our own "hacks," our secret tips that we're now sharing with you! Do you know how to make hot glue pliable again after it has cooled? What are the best tips for hot glue crafting with kids? How can you do more with hot glue than form blobs? We answer these questions and so many more in the project hacks.

As you go through the pages of this book, we hope you not only make some of the 50 designs we have shared, but that you are inspired to create even more with hot glue!

Glue Gun Basics

A glue gun is a handheld device that heats a glue stick to its melting point. The melting point varies depending on the type of glue stick and glue gun that you use. After cooling, the glue bonds various surfaces together. The glue gun is a handy tool in your craft arsenal because it is so fast—the gun heats up quickly and once applied, the glue is super quick to cool.

Always remember that a glue gun is HOT! Use caution and appropriate safety equipment when crafting. While we have done our best to mention all safety rules on each project, always use common sense and extreme caution when working with anything that is hot or sharp.

You can purchase a glue gun almost anywhere, from dollar stores to craft stores to hardware stores. However, you may find variety limited at brick and mortar stores. Widen your options by looking for specialty guns online.

Here are a few features that you may want to keep in mind when searching for the glue gun of your dreams.

The outer shell of the glue gun is designed to protect your hands from heat, but higher-temperature glue guns can still become warm to the touch. You never want to touch the tip (where the glue comes out of the gun) with your hand. Depending on the glue gun you purchase, there are a wide variety of tip options. Keep this in mind for your projects, as some tips offer more control over the flow and placement of the glue. Look for guns that say "detail" or "precision" on the packaging if you require this accuracy.

A high-quality glue gun will not drip continuously. There is a stopping mechanism that holds the glue behind the tip until the trigger is pulled. With these guns, you should only experience a small drip before the flow stops when not in use. Less expensive glue guns do not have this mechanism and allow the glue to drip continuously.

There are two main types of triggers. The first uses a single finger to activate and the second allows you to use your entire palm. People with diminished grip strength may want to shop for a glue gun with a larger trigger. Otherwise, choose whichever is more comfortable during your crafting.

You will insert your glue sticks into the back of the glue gun. There are mini- and full-size diameters, depending on which glue gun you purchase. Most color and glitter hot glue sticks come in only mini-size, so consider this when purchasing a hot glue gun.

Finally, you have the cord of your glue gun (or the lack of cord, in some cases). A cordless glue gun is a great option for crafting on the go or when you don't want to be hindered by a wall outlet.

Types of Glue Guns

The kind of glue gun you buy will depend on what projects you're working on. Variations in temperature, size, and precision are all factors to consider. Here's a look at some of what's on the market:

High-temp: These glue guns get up to 400°F, which produces a strong bond but can cause serious burns. Not recommended for use with children.

Low-temp: Sometimes you need a lower temperature. When dealing with foam or working with children or inexperienced crafters, be sure to pick up a low-temperature gun. Keep in mind that these get up to 120°F, so you'll still need to use caution.

Multi-temp: These are glue guns that can switch between low and high temp. If you are looking for a single glue gun for your craft room, this would be a great option.

Mini-size: If you want to use the mini-sized colored or glitter glue sticks, this is the perfect option.

Full-size: These are nice when using a large amount of hot glue, as you get more glue per stick.

Professional: Want to take it up a level? A pro gun is the way to go. From interchangeable tips to built-in stands, you will never want to go back after using one of these guns.

Specialty: From glue pens to glue pots, there are options on the market you may have never seen. Look for projects in this book using specialty equipment for ideas as to what these will do.

Pick and choose from the factors above to make your glue gun wish list. Basic guns start under $10 but the more specialized items are over $20. Want to go professional or get a big glue pot? You will be investing more than $50. Weigh your options and how much you will use the gun before purchasing. To create almost all of the projects in this book, a basic glue gun will suffice. However, some of the features mentioned above may make your crafting easier.

Types of Glue

Make sure you are purchasing the correct size and type of glue stick needed for your project. This will also depend on the type of glue gun you have purchased. These are some of the options available on the market today:

Clear: Standard glue sticks are fairly translucent but may not result in a clear appearance once used in a project. Also, these can yellow over time or when overheated.

High-temp: Gives a strong bond and is extremely hot.

Low-temp: Still requires caution, but perfect for working with kids.

Multi-temp: For use in both high- and low-temp guns.

Mini: For smaller-sized glue guns.

Full-size: For larger and professional guns.

Foam: Low or even ultra-low temp, used for gluing foam pieces together without melting the foam.

Glitter: Easily add sparkle to your projects.

Color: Perfect for making all sorts of decorative items from hot glue.

Scented: Add a special scent to your project.

Pro-Strength: Need extra strength? There's a glue stick for that!

Long: Tired of running out of glue? Try longer glue sticks and coiled glue.

No-String: Less likely to give strings, but we have had various levels of success.

Glow-in-the-dark: Spice up Halloween crafts or even every day projects.

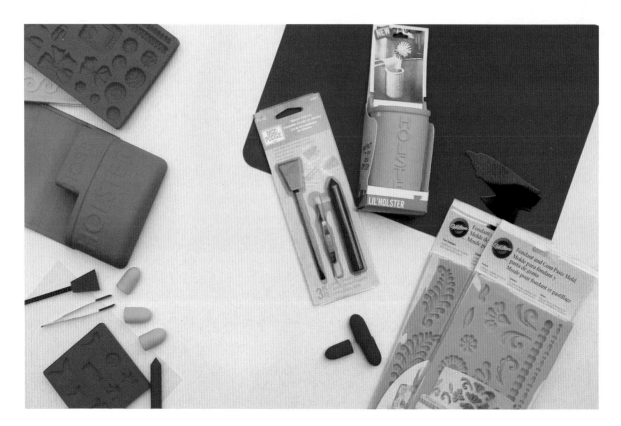

Glue Gun Accessories

Amp up your crafting with accessories that make crafting easier or safer. Find these items in the glue gun section, floral section, and even the baking aisle of your local craft store, or look online.

Silicone mats: These are a personal favorite and are used throughout this book. Use them to protect your work surface, catch drips, and even create unique crafts. Can't find one made for hot glue? Try the baking aisle to find a silicone mat or oven liner! Just be sure to mark any baking mats for crafting use only.

Finger Protectors: Slip these on the ends of your fingers when crafting to prevent hot glue burns.

Holders: A convenient way to keep your glue gun stored and out of the way. When shopping, look for hot glue gun holders that are heatproof, and hang one on your work table.

Silicone-Tipped Tools: Tired of burning your fingers when adding small embellishments? Try silicone-tipped tweezers and other tools made for this purpose.

Silicone Molds: Did you know that you can easily mold hot glue? Look for molds made for baking that can withstand high temperatures. Fondant molds are the perfect depth for most hot glue projects. Be sure to label them for crafting only after use.

Stands: Your glue gun may come with a stand attached. If it doesn't, look for stands you can purchase. You can also make your own hot glue gun stand (see page 83).

Tips: Look for glue guns that come with multiple interchangeable tips. Usually a pro gun will give you these options, allowing you to select the tip that is most appropriate for your project. Make sure your gun is completely cool before you handle the tip.

Glue Gun Expert Tips

You'll find specific hot glue hacks throughout this book, but here are a few universal pieces of wisdom that will help with any project.

- You'll find that when working on a project, the glue will often create strings as you move the tip. It's an unavoidable part of working with hot glue. To eliminate some strings, after you're done pressing the trigger, try moving the gun in a circular motion while pulling up. Once your project is complete, you can remove cooled strings by hand. If there are many, try gentle heat from a hair dryer or even a heat gun to melt the strings away. Don't apply too much heat, or you might melt your project!

- Hot glue can lose gloss or luster once it has been removed from a silicone mat or mold. The same texture that makes the glue easy to remove causes it to lose shine. Once the cooled project is removed, you can use a heat gun to gently warm the glue and return the shine. This is especially helpful with glitter glue.

- The tip of your glue gun can become extremely dirty with excess glue and gunk. Fortunately, cleaning your glue gun is super easy! Just turn it on and let it heat up. Then rub a ball of aluminum foil across the tip and other dirty areas. Consider wearing an oven mitt over your hand and use caution to not come in contact with the tip or any hot areas.

- Using colored glue? Unless you want a mixed effect, be sure to run the first color through the gun completely before going to the next color. You can discard leftovers or use a glue pot to re-melt blobs of glue to use on your next project. Watch for hacks throughout the book on making two-tone projects while switching between colored glues.

- Any tools that are coated with silicone make the glue easy to remove. Just peel up any cooled glue blobs. You can clean the silicone items with dish soap and water.

- Sometimes you want to redo a project or remove hot glue from a surface. Wait until the glue cools, then try peeling it up. This works best with hard surfaces like glass. If the glue won't budge, reheat it with a heat gun to make it easier to remove.

Fun for Kids

GLITTER CROWN

This royal crown is easy to make and fit for a king! Make the crown in sections then fit it to the size of your (or your kid's) head. Use gold or silver glitter hot glue sticks and gemstones of your choice to customize your royal headgear.

Supplies

Crown template (page 122)

Silicone mat

Glue gun of choice

Silver or gold glue sticks

Large acrylic gems

Instructions

1. Place the crown template under the silicone mat. Even with a colored mat, the lines should still be visible. Add the desired glitter glue sticks to your hot glue gun and heat to temperature.

2. The crown is made in 3-inch sections. The template has two sections. Measure the royal head to determine how many sections your crown will be.

3. Skipping the gemstone areas, trace the sections of the template with hot glue, then fill in one section at a time. Once a section is filled, add a gemstone. Complete two sections.

4. Allow to cool.

5. Remove the two sections from the silicone mat and shift to the left. Line up all the edges, then make a third section of the crown using the right side of the template. Allow to cool.

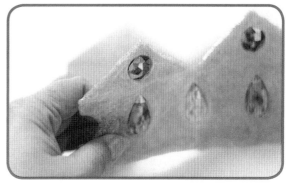

6. Repeat step 5 until you have enough sections to fit around the head.

7. Use hot glue to secure the two ends together. You may need to hold the crown ends together while the glue cools.

HACK: *Once a glitter glue stick has been used in a glue gun, it is extremely hard to get all the glitter out. You might find a sparkle or two of glitter weeks later. To prevent this, buy a second glue gun that's dedicated just to using glitter glue sticks.*

WINDOW CLINGS

Brighten up any room with window clings! Kids can let their imagination run wild by drawing with hot glue, then you can turn their creations into gorgeous window clings. Remember to use a low-temp hot glue when doing projects with kids.

Supplies

Low-temp glue gun

Multi-temp or low-temp colored glue sticks

Silicone mat

Finger guards (optional)

High-temp glue gun

High-temp clear glue sticks

Scissors

Instructions

1. Let the kids draw with the low-temp multi-colored glue on the mat, making sure they're wearing finger guards. Anything goes here, and they can let their imaginations run wild. Be sure to use an ultra-low-temp gun and supervise them closely, as the glue can still burn.

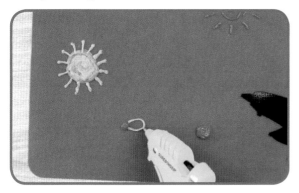

2. To minimize waste, allow them to use each color until it runs out by drawing images all over the mat.

3. An adult should take over for this step. Use a high-temp glue gun with clear glue sticks to cover each of the drawings with hot glue. Don't worry if the images are so close together that the hot glue bleeds from one to the next. You can cut them apart later if desired.

4. Allow everything to cool completely, then peel your window clings from the mat. You can cut any window clings apart with scissors.

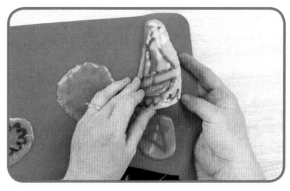

5. Use a little hot glue on the back of each cling to adhere to any window. The hot glue will release easily from the glass when you want to remove it later.

SUNCATCHER

A fun activity any time of the year is to make suncatchers with the kids. Did you know that you can actually use hot glue as your base? Low-temp hot glue is perfect for projects with the kids, and we've included some extra safety tips as well.

Supplies

Tissue paper

Scissors

Embroidery hoop

Silicone mat

Low-temp hot glue gun

Multi-temp or low-temp glue sticks

Finger guards (optional)

Silicone spatula

String

Instructions

1. Cut the tissue paper into squares or rectangles. We used pink and purple, but let your imagination run wild.

2. Separate the embroidery hoop into two pieces. You will only need the inner ring for this project.

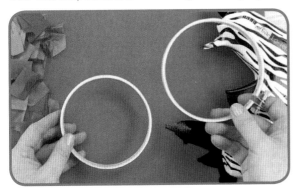

3. Place the hoop down on the silicone mat. Add low-temp glue to the inside of your hoop a little at a time. We recommend starting at the edges.

4. Spread the hot glue thin with a rubber spatula.

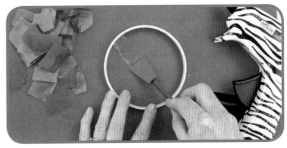

5. Using finger guards, if you'd like, stick random pieces of tissue paper into the glue while it is still slightly warm. Repeat until your entire hoop is filled.

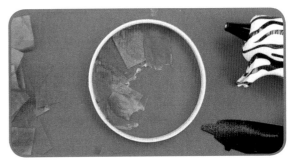

6. Allow to cool completely, then carefully lift from the silicone mat. Add a piece of string to the top. You may need to poke a hole in the glue/tissue paper to thread this through. Hang your suncatcher in a window and enjoy your creation!

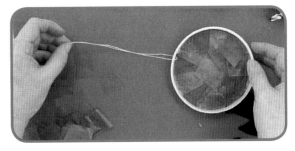

HACK: *Low-temp hot glue is still hot! Be sure to use caution and have the little ones wear finger protectors when doing these types of projects.*

GLOW-IN-THE-DARK SIGN

Do you have a little one who's afraid of the dark? Make a sign to put by their bed that glows in the dark. They will be comforted to sleep by the soft glow! You can make this one say anything you like, but "Sweet Dreams" is always a nice sentiment. Add additional embellishments to the sign if you wish.

Supplies

Silicone fondant molds in letter shapes

Glow-in-the-dark glue sticks

Glue gun of choice

Sign (a black background works best)

Instructions

1. Fill in the letter molds you need with glow-in-the-dark hot glue. To minimize air gaps, be sure to squeeze the hot glue into each corner of the mold.

2. Allow to cool completely, then pop out of the mold.

3. Arrange the letters on the sign as you work.

4. Use additional hot glue to secure the letters to the sign.

SPRING DAISIES

These daisies are easy to make and will brighten any room! Make a large bunch of daisies to fill a vase or just a few to add some cheer to a corner of your space.

Supplies

Silicone mat

Low-temp glue gun

White and pink low-temp glue sticks

Finger guards (optional)

Floral wire

Pliers

Instructions

1. About 1 inch from the edge of the mat, squeeze a dime-sized dollop of white glue onto the mat. Then extend a tapering line of glue down, making a teardrop shape. You can make a couple of teardrop shapes, one after the other.

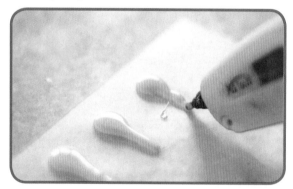

2. Before the shapes have cooled, fold over the silicone mat onto itself. Press down, starting at the point of the teardrop and extending to the large end. You can use your finger to push the glue toward the end. If the glue is too hot through the silicone mat, protect your fingers with the silicone finger guards.

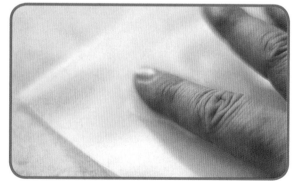

3. Allow the pieces to cool completely before lifting them off the mat. These will be the petals. Make five for each flower.

4. Wrap the end of the floral wire around the pliers three or four times.

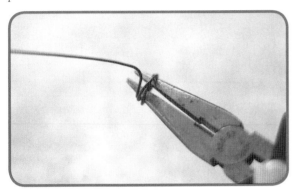

5. Switch the glue in the gun to the pink. Squeeze a dime-sized ball of pink glue onto the mat.

6. Place five petals on the pink glue while it is still warm.

7. Add another ball of pink glue to the top of the petals; this will be the back of the flower. Insert the coiled end of the wire into the glue. Add more glue to cover the coiled wire, if needed. You may need to hold the wire in place as the glue completely cools.

GLITTER DOTS MONOGRAM ART

Add a little bling to any room with a fun monogram made from glitter. Did you know that you can actually make dots of hot glue covered in glitter? It is so easy that even the kids will love this project. Remember that glitter is messy and this project should be completed somewhere that is easy to clean.

Supplies

Paint

Paint brush

Wood panel

Small disposable plastic cups

Glitter

Hot glue gun (high-temp for adults or low-temp for kids)

Glue sticks

Pencil

Letter stencil (optional)

Painter's tape or a lint roller (optional)

Instructions

1. Paint the wood panel and set aside to dry.

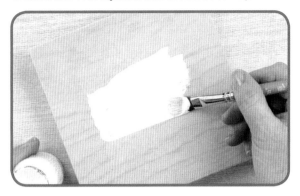

2. Fill a few disposable cups with glitter.

3. Drip the hot glue into the cups a few dots at a time. Shake the cups to cover the glue dots with glitter. This is a great place to get the kids involved if they would like to help and you don't want them touching hot glue.

4. Allow the dots to cool, then remove them from the glitter.

5. Continue until you have many dots of glitter for your monogram.

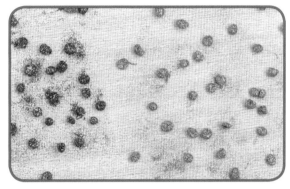

6. Draw a letter onto the wood panel or use a letter stencil to trace one.

7. Start with a line of hot glue on the letter outline.

8. Add dots of glitter to that line and continue until the entire letter is full.

9. You can use painter's tape or a lint roller on your project at the very end to remove excess glitter if desired.

EMBELLISHED MINT TIN

Use hot glue to smooth out the top of a mint tin so your child can embellish it! Once you have a smooth surface, it is the perfect surface for your child to paint or draw their own design. Then they can customize their tin with flowers, initials, or a special date before tucking their favorite small things inside.

Supplies

Glue gun of choice

Glue sticks

Empty mint tin

Spray paint

Paint pens

Instructions

1. Heat up the hot glue. Open the tin, then squeeze out the glue onto the top of the tin, extending to the sides, but being careful not to drip over the edges. No need to smooth by hand, hot glue is self-leveling when extremely hot. Allow to cool.

2. Spray paint the tin. Follow the instructions on the spray paint can.

3. Allow your child to decorate the top with paint pens.

HACK: *When you need a lot of glue to cover a large surface smoothly, use a glue gun that uses large glue sticks, and allow it to heat up for twice as long as you normally would.*

Home Decor Projects

EMBOSSED VASE

Add something special to any vase with a touch of hot glue. This technique for embossing on a clear vase is easy to do and can be done in minutes. Then you'll have a gorgeous vase for all your spring blooms. For this project, we recommend using a precision glue gun for making finer lines.

Supplies

Scissors

Embossed vase template (page 123)

Tape

Clear vase

Glue gun of choice

Glue sticks

Spray paint

Instructions

1. Start by cutting out the template and taping it to the inside of the glass vase.

HACK: *Not working with a clear vase? Look for transfer paper to transfer the image to your surface easily.*

2. Trace the template with hot glue. A glue gun marked as precision is best for projects like these. Allow the hot glue to cool completely.

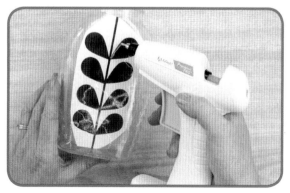

3. Paint over the entire vase with spray paint following the instructions on the can. Allow to dry, then enjoy in any room of your home.

HONEYCOMB BOWL

This sweet bowl is a fun knickknack to put on your side table or use in spring decor. Try using different colors or designs for different seasons.

Supplies

Tissue paper
Small glass bowl
Spray bottle filled with water

Glue gun of choice
Yellow glue compatible with your glue gun

Instructions

1. Wrap tissue paper around the bottom of the bowl, tucking any extra paper into the inside of the bowl.

2. Spray the tissue paper with water. Do not oversaturate—you want enough water to smooth the tissue to the bowl, but not so much that the tissue tears.

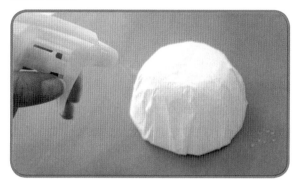

3. Starting in the center of the bowl, make a small circle with the yellow glue.

4. Moving outward, add more circles. Overlap the edges of the circles to keep them together.

5. Keep adding small circles around the bowl and down the sides. When you are done, set the bowl aside and allow the glue to cool completely.

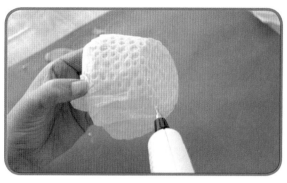

6. Once cool, the tissue paper and hot glue will easily peel away from the glass bowl. Rip the excess tissue from the top.

7. Get the remaining tissue very wet. The excess tissue can then be rubbed away with your fingers. You can also try scrubbing it away using a scrub brush, just use caution not to damage the bowl.

HACK: *The tissue paper allows the glue bowl to be easily removed from the glass bowl. With flat surfaces, coating the item with petroleum jelly works well, but for round surfaces, tissue paper prevents the glue from running down the sides, which can ruin your design.*

DIY LAMPSHADE

Add some style to your room with a hot glue lampshade! Use colored or glitter glue that matches your decor to make a statement piece. For extra fun, look for a lamp with a fillable base that you can use to store your extra glue sticks.

Supplies

Ruler

Permanent marker

Oven liner

Lamp (the lampshade can be damaged, but the lampshade wires must still be intact)

Glue gun of choice

Assorted colored glue sticks

Clear glue sticks

Instructions

1. Before taking apart your lampshade, measure the height and circumference. Draw a rectangle this size on the oven liner. If the oven liner is too small, you can tape a second oven liner or silicone mat on one end.

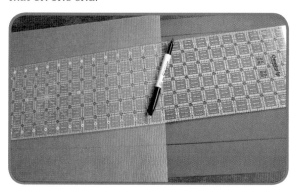

HACK: *An oven liner can be a great alternative to a silicone mat. They are inexpensive and often sold in larger sizes. However, an oven mat has a weave texture that transfers to your project, which means it is not an ideal alternative for all projects.*

2. Using a crisscross design, fill in the rectangle with different colors of glue. Switch to clear glue for the remaining steps.

3. Add stability to your lampshade by adding horizontal and vertical lines of glue. Use a ruler to keep them straight and even.

4. Remove the fabric lampshade from the lampshade wires.

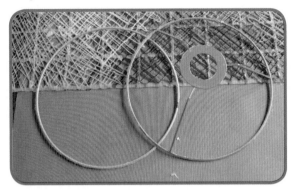

5. Glue the lampshade wires to the top and bottom of the rectangle, a few inches at a time, allowing the glue to set before moving to the next section.

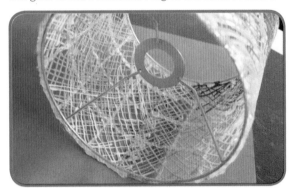

6. Add glue along the seam where the two ends of the rectangle meet, then add glue along the top and bottom edges as needed to secure in place.

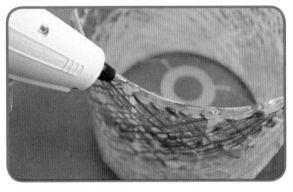

7. Put the lamp back together. Use a low-watt bulb to protect your hot glue lampshade from melting.

FAUX FERN

This faux fern looks so lifelike, you might find yourself watering it accidentally! But even with neglect, this is a potted plant that will stay beautifully green. If it gets dusty after sitting in a corner for months, just wash the leaves with soap and water to bring them back to life.

Supplies

18" floral wire stems

Jewelry pliers

Silicone mat

Glue gun of choice

Green hot glue

Styrofoam block (optional)

Instructions

1. Fold the floral wire stems in half and cut to form two pieces from each.

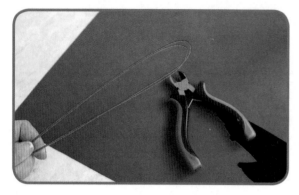

2. Use the pliers to straighten out the curved ends of the stems.

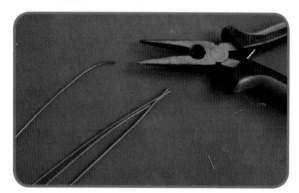

3. Lay out a row of stems on the silicone mat. Draw small leaf shapes down each wire with the glue, making sure one end of each leaf is in contact with the wire. The leaves should be about 1 inch apart and extend about two-thirds of the way down each stem.

4. Repeat, covering the whole mat with leafy stems.

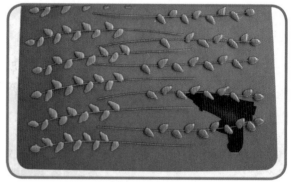

5. Place all the stems in a vase or decorative bucket. For more control over how your stems are displayed, place a Styrofoam block in the bottom of the container first, then poke the wire ends into the foam.

METALLIC ACCENTED CANDLES

Tired of plain candles in solid colors? Hot glue is the perfect way to dress them up! Add glue to the outside of candles for your home decor, parties, weddings, and more. Pick a stencil that goes with your theme and start adding glue.

Supplies

Candles

Stencil

Painter's tape

Precision hot glue gun

Metallic glue sticks

Instructions

1. Start by putting the stencil on your candle. Use painter's tape to hold it into place.

2. Go around the outer edge of each stencil opening with metallic hot glue. Do not touch the edge of the stencil with the glue; just use it as a guide. A precision glue gun will give you more control here.

3. Fill in the areas with hot glue as you work your way around the stencil.

4. Complete the stencil and allow the glue to cool.

5. Carefully pull back the stencil.

6. Add more embellishments to the candle if desired. Here, we added centers to each flower with a contrasting color of glue.

7. You can also trace around your stenciled glue to clean up the edges. Allow everything to cool before using the candle in your decor.

HACK: *Use a craft knife to cut away any glue that may have touched the stencil.*

FAIRY GARDEN WATERFALL

Fairy gardens are whimsical and can be a great addition to a porch or patio. You can add a waterfall to any fairy garden with just a few supplies and your hot glue gun. Your fairies will be so happy with the addition!

Supplies

Plastic canvas

Scissors

Clear plastic container

Three glue guns of choice

Clear glue sticks

Two shades of blue glue sticks

Clay pot

Skewer or dowel

Silicone mat

Instructions

1. Cut a strip from the plastic canvas as wide and long as you want the waterfall to be. Add clear glue to the bottom of the plastic container and stand the canvas in the glue, curving the top slightly. Hold in place while it cools.

2. Start building up the clear glue on the plastic canvas. You will need to add a little, wait until it cools, then add some more.

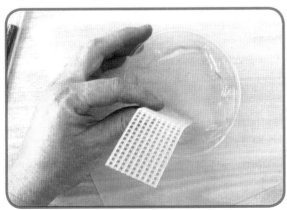

3. Glue the top edge of your plastic canvas to a clay pot. Continue to build the glue both in the plastic container and on the plastic canvas. Building it slowly will ensure that the plastic components do not melt.

4. Once the glue is built up, heat up all three glue guns. One should have clear glue and the other two should have two shades of blue glue. Then add drops of all three to the "pond" at once. While the glue is still warm, swirl with a skewer or dowel until you like the look of the "water."

5. Repeat step 4 on the waterfall itself. You will want to use any excess blue glue to build up the area where the waterfall meets the pond.

6. Use the same technique from step 4 to make one incoming and one outgoing stream, directly on top of the silicone mat. Let cool completely before lifting up.

7. Once everything is cool, add the components to your fairy garden. Add rocks around the clay pot to help hide it. Secure your streams into place with a little bit of additional clear glue.

EMBELLISHED PILLOW

Pillows are such an easy way to change up the look of a room with very little effort, but they can be expensive. Make this cute "hi" pillow in only a few minutes with the help of your glue gun. Thanks to Gina Luker of TheShabbyCreekCottage.com for this project.

Supplies

Blank pillow cover

Pencil

Glue gun of choice

Black glue sticks

Instructions

1. Start with a blank pillow cover. Make sure that it's ironed and ready to embellish. Sketch your word onto the fabric with a pencil. You could also use a printout from your computer as a guide if you would like.

2. Use black hot glue sticks and trace the lines, slowly and with even pressure, over your sketched-out guide. Let cool for at least an hour before filling with a pillow insert.

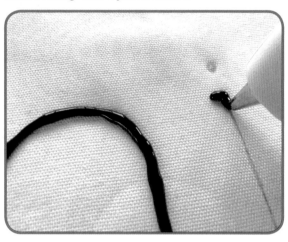

FUN FRAME FOR KIDS

This great craft was contributed to the book by Kara Rodgerson of MineForTheMaking.com. It's fun for not only adults but older kids too. Of course, always remember safety around a hot glue gun and be sure to unplug it when you're done using it!

Supplies

Glue gun (be sure to use low-temp when crafting with kids)
Colored glue sticks
Wooden craft frame

Instructions

1. Load the glue gun with a colored glue stick. After the gun has warmed up, draw hearts, polka dots, scallops, stripes, chevrons, etc., onto the frame. There are so many options!

3. When the hot glue has cooled, add a picture or piece of scrapbook paper to the inside of the frame. Now it's ready to display!

2. Switch out your glue sticks when you want to change colors. I usually discard leftover glue onto a paper plate so I can reload with the color I need. You can even go along the border of the frame or write words.

FLORAL ART DECOR

In this project by Jen Goode of 100Directions.com, you'll use your glue gun to create pretty floral art accents. Decorate a frame or create mini decor pieces in just a few steps. Add a splash of color or create white-on-white designs.

Supplies

Pencil

Wood frame

Low-temp or multi-temp hot glue gun

Glue sticks of choice

White paint or white chalk paint (optional)

Paint brush(es)

Water color paints (optional)

Decoupage medium (optional)

Instructions

1. Using a pencil, sketch out the design you'd like to create. Leave plenty of room for the thickness of the hot glue in your line art.

2. Using the low heat setting, trace over the pencil lines. Move slowly to better control the thickness of the glue lines. You can layer lines as the glue cools to add more depth to your design as well.

3. Apply one or two coats of white paint to the frame if desired. If you are using watercolors in the next step, be sure to use chalk paint here. Allow to dry between paint layers.

4. Optionally, you can use watercolor paints to add pretty painted color to your hot glue art. The chalk paint allows for the color to be absorbed.

5. Seal your art piece with decoupage medium if you'd like.

MASON JAR LID WREATH

Faux succulents are one of my favorite things to craft with. I love adding their bright colors and interesting shapes to planters, frames, and wreaths. That is why I was so excited when I found that I could make my own faux succulents with glue and a silicone fondant mold! Hang a mini wreath in a kitchen window, use them as place cards at a wedding shower, or tie one onto a gift in place of a traditional bow! Project by Jessica Hill of MadInCrafts.com.

Supplies

Silicone fondant mold in a succulent shape

High-temp glue gun

Hot glue sticks (I prefer the extra-long sticks)

Green acrylic paint

Paintbrush

Mason jar ring

Twine

Scissors

Instructions

1. Start by filling the silicone mold with hot glue. Use the tip of the glue gun to make sure you are filling in all the cavities in the mold. To minimize air gaps, be sure to squeeze the hot glue into each corner of the mold.

2. Allow the glue to fully cool, then pop it out of the mold. Repeat to make as many succulents as you would like. Paint the succulents with the acrylic paint. Experiment with adding colors to the ends of each leaf to mimic the look of real succulents. Allow the paint to fully dry.

3. Place a small drop of hot glue on the outer edge of the mason jar ring. Carefully place the end of a long piece of twine on the glue. Then wrap the ring two or three times with the twine. Secure the end with more glue and trim away the excess. Add a small hanging loop to the wreath with more twine.

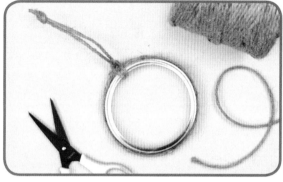

4. Position the faux succulents on the bottom of the wreath. Secure them in place with additional hot glue.

DIY PLANTER

Need a planter for a flower, or even some succulents? Why not make one out of hot glue? Yes, you can actually make an entire planter out of hot glue and add any embellishment you can dream of to the front.

Supplies

Glue gun of choice

Glue sticks of choice

Clay pot

Petroleum jelly (optional)

Silicone mat

Outdoor paint

Paint brush

Instructions

1. Start by applying your glue to the clay pot. You can cover the clay pot in petroleum jelly to make the glue easier to remove once complete.

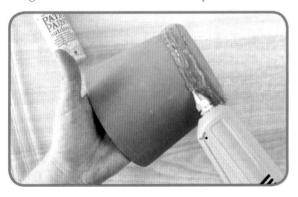

2. Apply one layer of glue then go back and apply a thick second layer. Do not cover the bottom of the pot.

3. Use glue to create any embellishment you would like on the front of your planter. Here we added a cactus shape.

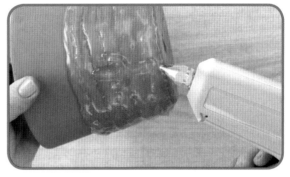

4. Allow to cool completely then remove the glue from the clay pot. You can use a long flat object to aid in removal like the handle of a paint brush.

5. Remove the planter completely.

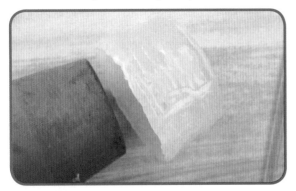

6. Set your bottomless planter down onto a silicone mat. Add glue to the bottom of the planter, making sure to glue all the way around the sides.

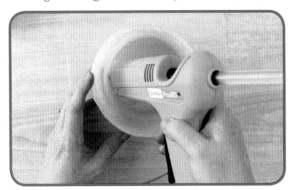

7. Add two more layers to the bottom for additional support. You can also leave a hole in the center for drainage.

8. Use a good-quality outdoor paint and paint brush to paint the entire planter. Add contrasting colors to your embellishments if desired.

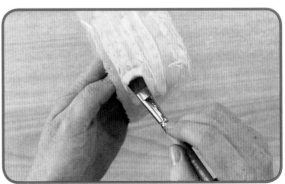

Holiday Favorites

GLITTERY CHRISTMAS ORNAMENTS

Decorate your tree with hot glue! These simple ornaments are easy to make with your glue gun and some glitter glue sticks. Make solid ornaments or even turn them into frames for your favorite pictures. Use our template for example shapes or make your own templates in any shape you love.

Supplies

Silicone mat

Christmas ornament templates (page 124)

Glue gun of choice

Glitter glue sticks

String

Scissors

Finger guards

Instructions

1. Start by laying the silicone mat over the template. Add glitter glue to your glue gun in the color desired and heat to temperature. Once heated, remove any previous glue that is in your gun by squeezing onto the mat. Once the glitter glue starts to come out, you can continue with your project.

2. Cut a piece of string with the scissors. Use your glue gun to add the string to the nonstick mat at the top of the ornament.

3. Start adding hot glue around the outer edge of the ornaments, making sure that the mat does not move on the template. You can expect to use about 1½ glue sticks per ornament.

4. Continue filling in the entire ornament with the glitter glue.

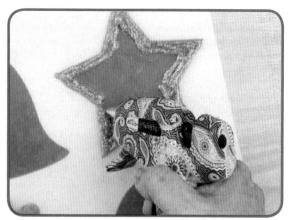

5. Use a finger guard to smooth out any imperfections in the glue while still hot.

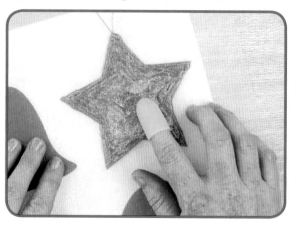

6. Be sure to remove one color of glue from your gun before starting on another color.

HACK: *One way to transition from one color to another using the same glue gun is to add rings around one of the ornaments to create a frame. You can do this with any of the shapes, but we show the oval here.*

7. Allow the ornaments to cool completely before peeling up from the nonstick mat. Hang them on your tree as is, or add a picture using a little more hot glue for the frame ornament.

DECORATED CHRISTMAS CARDS

Make any Christmas card extra special with a bit of glue and a glue gun. Here we used plain cards, but you can also add a three-dimensional effect to pre-decorated store-bought cards in a similar manner.

Supplies

Cards
Paper cutouts (optional)
Color and glitter glue sticks
Glue gun of choice

Instructions

1. Add paper cutouts to plain cards if desired. Then, start layering on hot glue accents in a variety of shapes. You can really let your imagination run wild!

2. Repeat until you are happy with the card, then allow to cool. Stuff into an envelope and send off to family and friends. Be sure to check with your post office to see if extra postage is required.

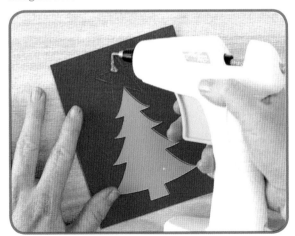

CHRISTMAS DOILY

Add a Christmas doily to your decor this holiday season. It is so easy to make with a few different colors of glitter glue and some imagination.

Supplies

Cookie cutter or paper cutout
Pencil
Silicone mat

Glue gun of choice
Glitter glue sticks

Instructions

1. Use a pencil to trace a cookie cutter or paper cutout onto the silicone mat. Arrange in such a way that a circle doily will be made.

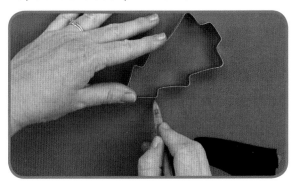

HACK: Tracing onto the mat gives you guide lines for your hot glue. The marks can be erased later with a Magic Eraser.

2. Use glitter glue to trace the lines that were drawn with pencil.

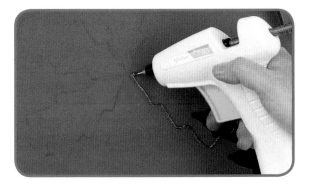

3. Add additional detail with hot glue if desired.

4. Start filling in outside areas with additional glitter glue.

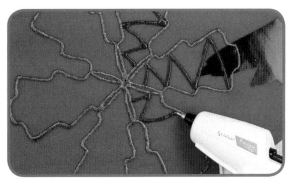

5. Continue until you have filled in all the open areas. This will help to hold your doily together.

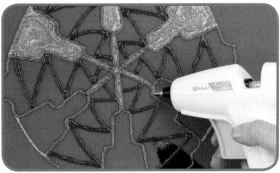

6. Finish by filling in the remainder of the doily with glue.

7. Allow to cool completely on the mat.

8. Peel up the cooled doily and then use in your home decor.

FALL LEAVES WREATH

Add this stunning modern wreath to your home this fall. Would you believe that those leaves are painted hot glue? Your guests won't believe it either!

Supplies

High-temp glue gun or glue skillet

High-temp glue sticks

Silicone mat

Scissors

Embroidery hoop

Metallic paint in a variety of shades

Ribbon

Instructions

1. Start by squeezing out as much hot glue as possible onto your mat before the gun gets hard to squeeze. Alternately, you can melt several sticks in a glue skillet and use a spoon to add the glue to your mat.

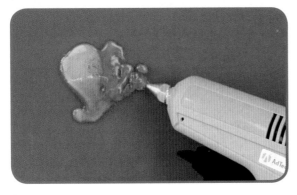

2. While the glue is still hot, fold the mat over and press the glue flat.

3. Allow to cool completely then pull back the mat.

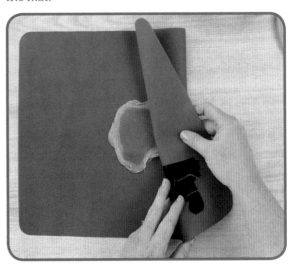

4. Peel the hot glue sheet from the mat.

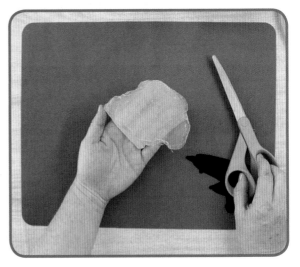

HACK: *Sheets of hot glue like this can be used in a wide variety of ways. Cut into any shape you desire and then paint!*

5. Cut into several leaf shapes with your scissors.

6. Remove the inner ring from the embroidery hoop and paint with a metallic paint on all sides.

7. Paint the hot glue leaves with a few different colors of metallic paint.

8. Once your paint is completely dry, add the leaves to the hoop with a bit of hot glue. Hang with a piece of ribbon.

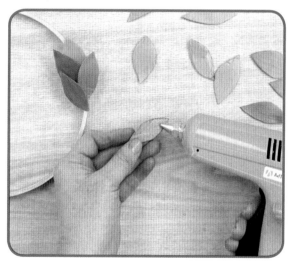

BLOODY MASON JARS FOR HALLOWEEN

Add some fright to your home for Halloween night by making a set of these bloody mason jars. This quick and easy project is perfect for adding to a spooky mantel or haunted house.

Supplies

2 glue guns of choice

2 shades of red glue sticks

Red mason jars

Tea candles

Instructions

1. Add two different shades of red glue to two separate glue guns. Work your way around the top of the jar with both glue guns at the same time, dripping glue and letting the shades mix. Allow to cool then put a candle in the jar.

DECORATIVE EASTER EGGS

Plain plastic Easter eggs can become something special with just a little glue and spray paint. Add some of these eggs to your decor this spring for an elegant addition to your home.

Supplies

Precision glue gun

Glue sticks of choice

Plastic Easter eggs

Spray paint in the color of your choice

Instructions

1. While the two halves of the egg are together, add glue around the seam where the pieces join. This will ensure that they stay together once your project is complete.

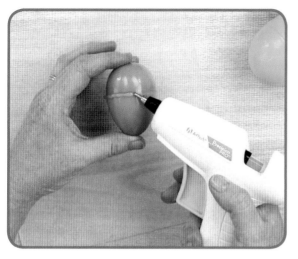

2. Add a variety of embellishments to your eggs using a hot glue gun. A precision gun works best for projects like these.

HACK: *Since you'll be painting the eggs, using up leftover color or glitter glue in your gun works great.*

3. Once the glue has cooled, paint all sides with spray paint according to the instructions on the can and then allow to dry before adding to your home decor.

WARTY PUMPKINS

These days it seems like the uglier the pumpkin, the better. Did you know that you can turn a cute, inexpensive plastic pumpkin into something trendy with hot glue? See how to make those warty pumpkins then make a batch for your home this fall.

Supplies

Foam or plastic pumpkins

Glue gun of choice

Glue sticks of choice

Wood dowels (optional)

Orange craft paint

Green craft paint (optional)

Paint brush

Instructions

1. Remove the pumpkin stem if possible and set aside.

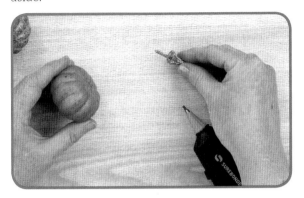

2. Layer on blobs of hot glue to create the rustic texture on the pumpkin.

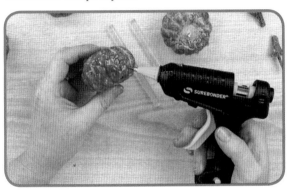

HACK: *Work on multiple pieces at once to create layers. Allow the hot glue to cool on your first piece while you move on to more. This makes it easier to build up the hot glue.*

3. Once you are happy with your warts, it is time to paint. You can add a dowel rod to the pumpkin stem hole if desired to give you something to hold while painting. While the pumpkin dries, add the dowel to a jar to hold upright. Paint on a light coat of orange paint and then return with a few touches of green if desired to create a layered effect.

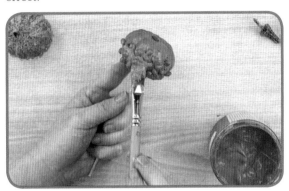

TWINKLE LIGHTS

Add a little sparkle to your holidays with these festive twinkle lights! Use them as part of a Christmas centerpiece or to add some sparkle to your Fourth of July barbecue.

Supplies
Battery-operated LED lights (with batteries)
Silicone mat
Glue gun of your choice
Glitter glue

Instructions
1. Lay the lights as flat as possible on the silicone mat. This may need to be done in sections. With the glue, draw stars on the LED lights and midway between each of the LED lights. Allow to cool.

2. Peel the stars up from the mat. Turn over and use the glue to fill in the back of each star as well.

3. Turn on the lights to test. The combination of lit and unlit stars adds extra sparkle.

NAUTICAL MASON JARS

Add a few embellishments to a mason jar for a nautical themed jar that is perfect for summer. You can also add a grid top to the jar to keep it in your beach-themed bathroom throughout the year to hold toothbrushes.

Supplies

Nautical-themed silicone fondant mold

High-temp glue gun

Hot glue sticks

Craft paint

Paint brush

Spray paint

Mason jar

Instructions

1. Start by filling the mold with hot glue. To minimize air gaps, be sure to squeeze glue into each corner of the mold.

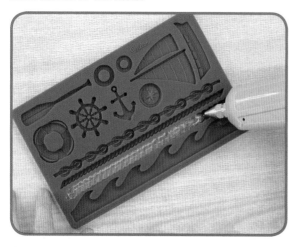

2. Allow to cool completely then remove from the mold.

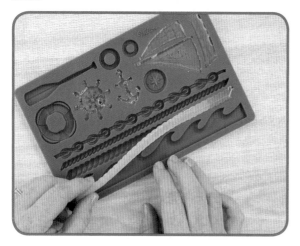

HACK: *You can use a pair of scissors to trim away at the edges if they look unfinished.*

3. Paint the pieces with a few coats of craft paint. Use as many colors as you desire. Allow to dry.

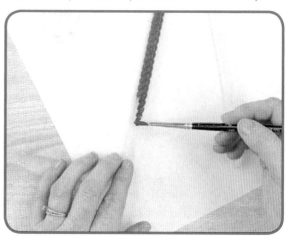

4. In the meantime, spray paint the jar according to the directions on the can. Once everything is dry, use additional hot glue to add the embellishments to the mason jar.

Glue Gun Hacks

CUSTOM STENCILS

Create any stencil you can imagine with a bit of glue. Then add your design to shirts, tote bags, aprons, and more. Imagine all of the possibilities for creating your own fashions!

Supplies

Silicone mat

Glue gun of choice

Glue sticks of choice

Object to trace (optional)

Stencil spray fabric paint

Shirts, tote bags, or any other fabric object

Instructions

1. Start by drawing any shape you like onto the surface of the silicone mat.

2. You can trace any object you have around your home to create a stencil. Remember that the color of the glue does not matter in this case.

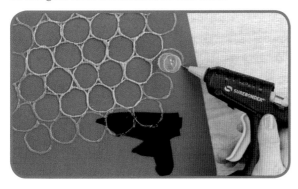

3. Allow your stencil to cool completely on the mat then peel up to remove.

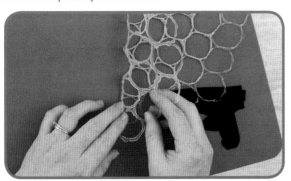

4. You can create your stencil in a wide variety of shapes and sizes depending on your final project. Here we even traced around a cookie cutter to create a star.

5. Once your stencil is complete, lay it on top of your shirt or other fabric. Then spray with the stencil spray.

6. Pick up the stencil to reveal your design.

HOT GLUE ETCHING

Use glue as a resist when etching glass. The glue gives great curves and organic lines that you can't get when using a glass etching stencil. You can use this technique to etch initials or dates into glasses for special occasions.

Supplies

Glass surface

Glue gun of choice

Glue sticks of choice

Etching cream

Paintbrush

Instructions

1. Add your design to the glass with glue. Allow to cool.

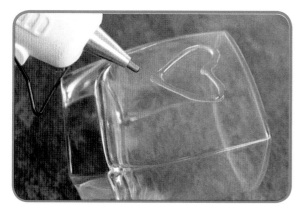

2. Following the manufacturer's instructions, apply the etching cream. Allow to sit for the required amount of time.

3. Continuing to follow the manufacturer's instructions, rinse away the etching cream. If some of the glue comes off at this point, that is okay.

4. Remove the rest of the glue, rinse away any remaining etching cream, and allow the glass to dry.

STAMPED FABRIC PILLOW

In this project by Carissa Bonham of CreativeGreenLiving.com, you can use hot glue to make a stamp. You can then use your hot glue stamp to add a fun design to a pillow. This stamped pillow is perfect for a teen room, but the possibilities are endless!

Supplies

Glue gun of choice

Glue sticks of choice

Lid from an empty metal can

Wine cork

Pillow case

Scrap paper or cardboard

Paper plate or other palette

Soft fabric paint or fabric ink

Soft sponge brush

Instructions

1. Create a stamp by using your glue gun to draw a heart, or any other shape, on the can lid. To stay safe, I used a smooth-edge can opener to remove the lid so there were no sharp edges. Allow glue to cool.

HACK: *If the glue coming out of your glue gun spreads too much, try unplugging the glue gun. As you continue to work without the glue gun continuing to heat up, the glue coming out will be more solid and give more texture to your stamp.*

2. Once the glue on this side is completely cool, use hot glue to adhere a wine cork to the other side of the lid to serve as a handle.

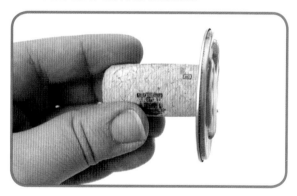

3. Prepare your pillowcase by ironing it to remove any creases. If the fabric feels very stiff, you may achieve better results by first washing and drying the pillowcase in order to remove any starch used during the manufacturing process. To prevent the fabric ink from bleeding through, line the inside of the pillowcase with a double layer of scrap paper or cardboard. Place the pillowcase on a hard, smooth surface such as a table for stamping.

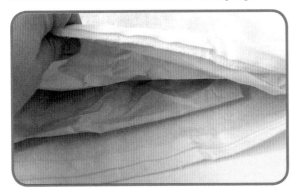

4. Fill your paper plate or palette with the desired colors of fabric paint or ink. Use the sponge brush to dab it onto your stamp. Blot away excess ink with a paper towel, if needed, before stamping onto the pillowcase. You may want to try a few test stamps on scrap fabric first if you are new to fabric stamping.

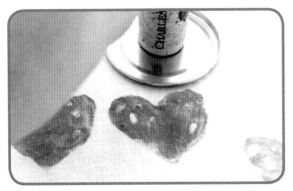

5. To create the rainbow heart effect, I started by stamping purple hearts in the lower left corner, then continued with other colors across the pillow until the whole thing was filled. Allow to dry completely. Heat set if needed following the instructions for the brand of fabric ink or paint used.

MAKING MOLDS WITH HOT GLUE

Making molds has never been easier or cheaper! You can turn hot glue into a mold for soaps and other crafts in just minutes. Pick a simple object to start with, then work your way up to more complicated creations.

Supplies

Object to mold (needs to be able to withstand the heat of hot glue)

Disposable paper cup

Petroleum jelly

High-temp glue gun or glue skillet

High-temp glue sticks

Craft knife

Pliers (optional)

Instructions

1. Start by coating your object as well as the inside of the paper cup in petroleum jelly. We recommend a fairly simple object for maximum success.

2. Add enough hot glue to the paper cup so that it will completely surround your object. You want to make sure the object will not be able to touch the sides or bottom of the cup. Here you can use your high-temp glue gun or a glue skillet to melt enough glue for the mold.

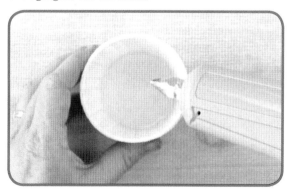

3. Allow the glue to cool for 10 to 20 seconds.

4. Add the object to the glue in the cup, making sure it does not sink to the bottom but is far enough in the glue to create the shape you desire. Set aside and allow to cool completely.

5. Remove any excess glue from around the top of the object with a craft knife.

6. Peel back the paper cup and discard.

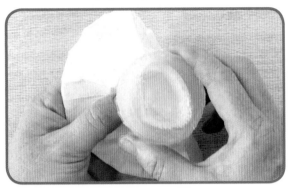

7. Remove the object from the mold. You can use pliers here if needed.

8. Your mold is now ready for pouring in soap or making other crafts.

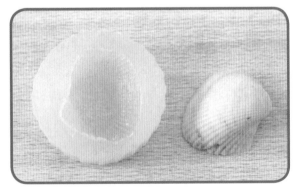

GLUE GUN STAND

Not all glue guns come with a built-in stand. Some come with a wire stand that can get lost or are removed when they get in the way. And all glue guns need a safe place to drip when they are not being used.

Supplies

Wire cutters

Wire coat hanger

Pliers

Piece of wood for base

Drill

Glue gun of choice

Glue sticks of choice

Instructions

1. Using wire cutters, cut a section of the wire coat hanger.

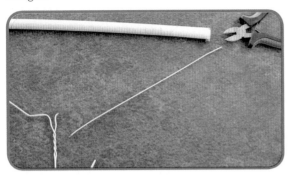

2. Using pliers, bend the wire into an "M" shape.

3. Remove any plastic coating from the middle section of the M.

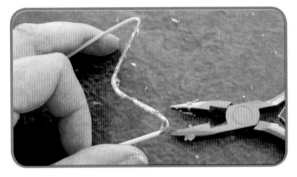

4. Position the wire on the wood. Cut down the length of the wire for smaller glue guns, if needed. Mark where the bottom ends of the wire touch the wood.

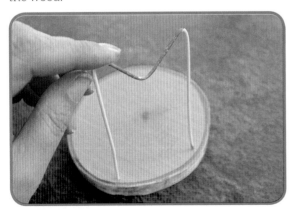

5. Drill small holes where you marked the wood in step 4.

6. Put a dot of glue into each hole, then insert the ends of the wire. Hold until the glue has set.

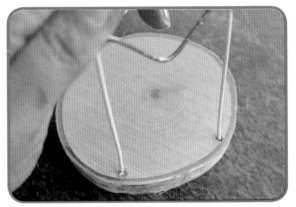

FAUX WAX ENVELOPE SEALS

Add a formal touch to the outside of an envelope with this faux wax seal! Using a metal stamp or ring designed to imprint into wax and some bright-red hot glue, you can create this iconic look in just a few seconds!

Supplies

Glue gun of choice
Red glue sticks
Envelopes
Metal Stamp

Instructions

1. Create a dollop of red glue on the seam of the envelope.

2. Firmly press the metal stamp into the glue. Do not pull it out. Allow the stamp to sit in the glue while it cools.

3. Once the glue has cooled for a few minutes, carefully remove the stamp.

REALISTIC LOOKING GEODES

Fool your friends and family with these realistic looking geodes! Though lighter in weight than the natural stones they mimic, these geodes are just as pretty!

Supplies

Pencil

Paper-mâché egg

Craft knife

Faux concrete paint

Paintbrush

Scissors

Large glue sticks

Paper towel

Purple color shift paint

Glue gun of choice

Purple glitter glue sticks

Tweezers (optional)

Instructions

1. Draw a line around the middle of the paper mâché egg.

2. Using the craft knife, carefully cut around the egg on the line. Keep the rounded-bottom half of the egg. Discard the pointy half of the egg.

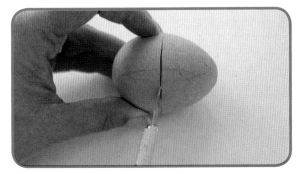

3. Paint the outside of the egg half with the faux concrete paint. Set aside to dry.

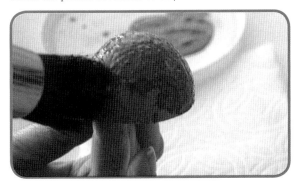

4. Using scissors, carefully cut the large glue sticks into small "crystals."

5. Put the glue crystals on a paper towel. Drizzle with purple color shift paint. Rub in the paint with a paper towel, rubbing off the excess.

6. Lay out the crystals to dry.

7. Load your glue gun with the purple glitter glue stick. Starting at the bottom of the egg, add a dollop of glue and start placing the crystals. If you have trouble placing them with your fingers, use tweezers to get into the small spaces.

8. Keep adding more crystals, aiming the points of each crystal towards the middle for a realistic look.

9. Once the geode is full of crystals and has cooled, add a rim of glitter glue around the edge.

10. Before the glitter glue rim has a chance to cool, flip the geode over onto the silicone mat and press down. Allow to cool.

11. Once the geode has cooled, peel it up off the mat. You can carefully use a heat gun to heat the glitter edges, which will bring back the shine.

HACK: *You can paint hot glue using multi-surface paints to create the look of different colored crystals. In this project, we used purple for an amethyst look, but green, blue, and red would work to create peridot, sapphire, and ruby faux crystals!*

Jewelry and Accessories

FAUX OPAL EARRINGS

These earrings look like opals, but cost a fraction of the price! They are easy to make in just a few minutes. These earrings make great thank-you gifts, party favors, or something fun to make for yourself! Earring posts are available in the jewelry section of the craft store.

Supplies

Earring posts
Styrofoam block
Glue gun of your choice
Iridescent glitter glue sticks of your choice

Instructions

1. Take the backs off of the earring posts. Now gently push the earring posts into the Styrofoam. Don't push it all the way down, since you don't want the glue to melt the Styrofoam.

2. Squeeze hot glue onto center of earring post. Slowly squeeze more out until the glue dollop fills the earring base. Allow to cool.

TWO-TONE NECKLACE CHARM

Inexpensive, lightweight, and makes an impact! This fun necklace charm takes only a few minutes to make but has a whole lot of "wow!"

Supplies

Glue gun of choice

Two colors of glitter glue sticks

Bezel

Silicone mat

Instructions

1. Discarding the glue that comes from the tip, feed the first glue stick through the glue gun until squeezing the trigger no longer advances the glue. Add the second color glue stick.

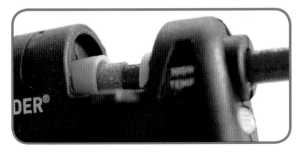

2. Continue to feed the glue stick in, about 10 more squeezes.

3. Place the bezel on the silicone mat. Starting at the bottom of the bezel, create a large dollop of glue.

4. If after about four squeezes, the new color has not shown up yet, squeeze off excess glue on the edge of the mat until the second color appears. Then continue adding to the large dollop on the bezel. Keep adding until the circle reaches the top of the bezel, then stop. Allow to cool.

HACK: *Using two colors of glitter adds dimension to this simple pendant. Allowing the colors to run together gives it a "natural" look.*

HOT GLUE SANDALS

Yes, you can make functional shoes using hot glue that are comfortable enough to wear! These hot glue sandals are functional and stylish. Your friends won't believe that you made these shoes yourself—out of glue!

Supplies

Glue skillet

Standard glue sticks (about 50 mini glue sticks per shoe)

Shoe to trace

2 silicone mats

Permanent marker

Glue gun(s) of choice

Colored glue sticks of choice

2 buttons, each with 2 holes

Metal spoon (use a spoon that can be dedicated to the glue skillet—you may never get all the glue off of the spoon)

Book (must be larger than the shoe)

Cotton swabs

Rubbing alcohol

Measuring tape or ruler

Perle cotton or string

Large eye needle (such as a tapestry needle)

Instructions

1. Fill the glue skillet with glue sticks and allow the glue to melt. Once the glue is almost melted, lower the heat. You don't want the glue to scorch or burn—this would give the glue a yellowish tint.

Hack: *Using a glue skillet allows you to heat a lot of glue at once, which is essential for a project like this where you want one solid block of glue for the sole of the shoe.*

2. Trace the shoe onto a silicone mat using the permanent marker. These shoes are made in reverse—if you're tracing the right shoe, you will be making the left shoe.

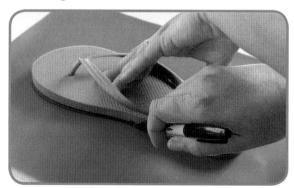

3. If you are using our same flower design, make colored glue dots on the mat for the flower centers.

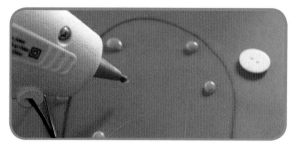

4. Add a big dollop of clear glue at the inside of the base of the big toe, and put in a button.

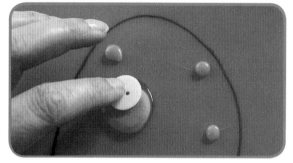

5. Using the purple glue, add the petals to the flowers. Extend them past the shoe border to keep the design interesting.

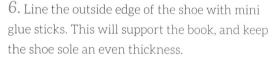

6. Line the outside edge of the shoe with mini glue sticks. This will support the book, and keep the shoe sole an even thickness.

7. Once the glue skillet has completely melted the glue sticks, use the spoon to pour large dollops of the glue onto the silicone mat. Make sure there is enough glue to cover the entire surface of the shoe.

8. Lay the second silicone mat on top of the first. Put the book on top of the second mat, and gently press down. The glue sticks along the borders should help to keep the book from being pressed down too far.

9. Leave the sole of the shoe to cool completely. If you have two more silicone mats, you can get started on the second shoe.

10. Once the glue has cooled, remove the glue from the mats. The permanent marker will stick to the glue, providing you with an outline to cut around. Once you have cut out the shoe, you can use cotton swabs and rubbing alcohol to remove any lines that are still left along the edge.

11. Trace two edges of the book onto the mat to make an L shape. Draw another L shape a couple inches away from the first.

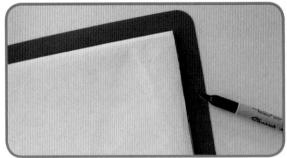

12. Measure the length of the straps on the sandal you traced. For US women's size 8 shoe, the strap length is about 6 inches. Mark this length on both arms of both L shapes. When in doubt, make the straps longer—you can always cut them shorter later.

13. Trace the L shapes with glue to make the straps.

14. Using the hot tip of your glue gun, push into the sole to expose both holes of the button. Do this on both sides of the sole. On the bottom of the sole, soften the glue between the two holes as well.

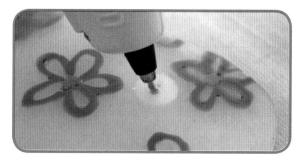

15. Thread the large-eye needle with about 15 inches of perle cotton or string, with the needle in the middle so the two thread tails are about the same length. Use the needle to bring the thread from the top of the shoe down to the bottom through one button hole, and then back up the other side through the other hole.

16. Place a dab of glue on the bottom of the sole to fill the area where you softened the glue, then press onto the silicone mat to flatten.

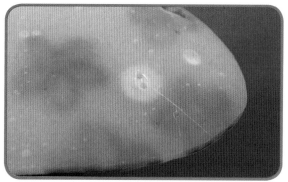

17. With the same color glue you used to make the straps, cover the strings, starting from the top of the sole and extending up about 1 inch for an adult female shoe. This height will have to be adjusted based on the height of the toes of the person wearing the shoes (larger for a large man, smaller for a child's foot). Allow to cool.

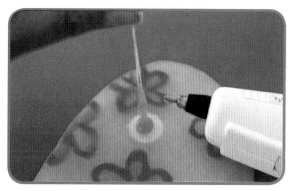

18. Remove the now cooled sandal straps from the silicone mat. Place the corner up against the glue strings you have built up.

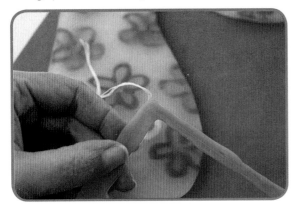

19. Extend the two threads in each direction along the strap. Secure with glue, then cover completely with glue. Make sure this side is very smooth, as this will be the side touching the skin of your foot.

20. Secure the ends of the strap toward the back of the shoe, past the arch. You can customize the fit by trying on the shoe to see where the strap ends feel most comfortable. If the straps are too long, trim off the excess with scissors before gluing the strap in place.

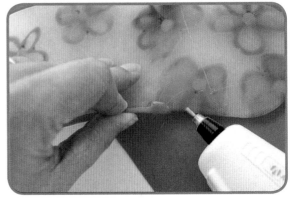

21. Add glue as needed where the angle of the strap meets the base. Cover any exposed string, and add any support needed.

22. Complete these steps for the second shoe. Be careful that you do not create two right shoes or two left shoes!

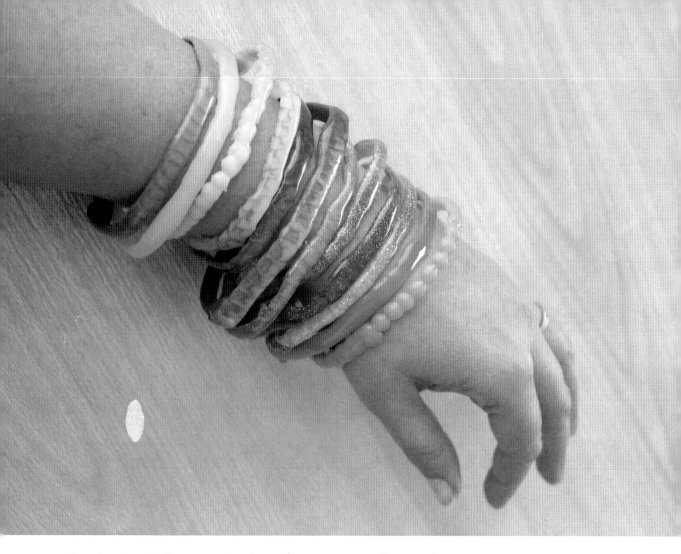

STYLISH BANGLE BRACELETS

This is a fun way to use glue when you're changing your glue gun from one color to the next. Set aside the long strands, then easily turn them into fashionable bangles in just a few steps!

Supplies

Glue gun of choice

Glue sticks in various colors

Silicone mat

Scissors

Instructions

1. Create a line of glue by squeezing out one "pearl" after another, allowing them to touch. This works great when switching glue from one color to another. Make sure the line of glue pearls is long enough to extend around your wrist. You can use the edge of the silicone mat as a guide to keep your line straight.

2. Allow to cool, but not harden, before peeling from the mat. Collect as many of these lines of glue as you like.

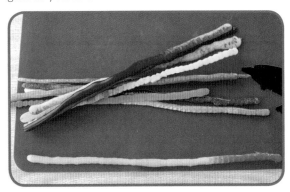

3. Measure the bangle around your hand. Don't just measure your wrist—the bangle needs to be large enough to slip on and off your hand. Cut to length with scissors.

4. Using the hot tip of the glue gun, melt the top of one side of the line of glue, and the bottom of the other side of the line of glue.

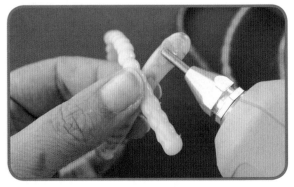

5. Press the melted sides together to fuse them. Allow to cool.

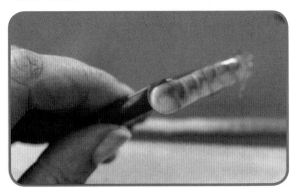

6. Try on your bangle to check the fit. Make as many bangles as you like!

SEASHELL HAIR PINS

Use molds to create custom hair pins for any occasion! A handful of seashell-themed hair pins form the perfect mermaid crown here. Make custom hair pins for the flower girl at a wedding, for a themed birthday party, or just for fun!

Supplies

High-temp glue gun

Silicone fondant mold

Bobby pins

Assorted colors of hot glue sticks

Instructions

1. Using a very hot glue gun, fill the cavity of the mold with the desired color. To minimize air gaps, be sure to squeeze glue into each corner of the mold.

2. Dip the bent end of the bobby pin into the glue in the mold, about ½ inch from the edge.

3. Rotate the bobby pin two or three times to ensure the end is coated in glue.

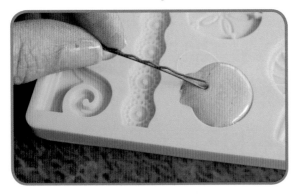

4. Lay the bobby pin down and allow the glue to cool.

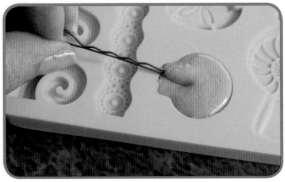

5. While you allow the glue to cool, you can make more pins using the other designs in the mold.

6. Once the glue has cooled, lift up on the bobby pins to remove the glue from the molds.

HACK: *If you know you want a large variety of colors, cut your glue sticks! Only insert half of a glue stick into the gun, and save the other half for a future project. This prevents you from wasting glue as you advance the glue stick to get to the next color.*

GLOW-IN-THE-DARK EMBELLISHED SHOES

Make some glow-in-the-dark shoes for a party or fun event in just minutes. These shoes look like regular shoes in the daylight but as soon as the lights go out, they are tons of fun! Surprise your friends and light up the night.

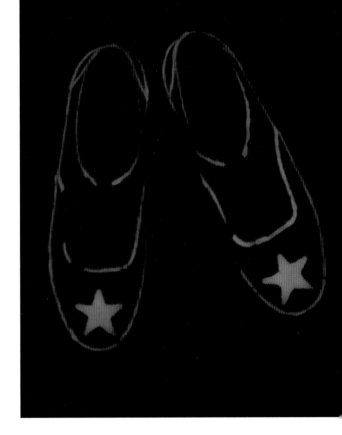

Supplies

Glue gun of choice
Glow-in-the-dark glue sticks
Plain tennis shoes

Instructions

1. Using the glue gun filled with glow-in-the-dark glue, draw lines of hot glue on all of the shoe seams.

2. You can also draw on shapes or additional lines for even more glow-in-the-dark fun. Allow the glue to cool completely before wearing your shoes.

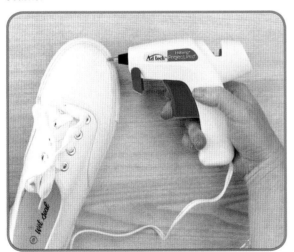

COLORFUL WATCH BAND

When you make your own watch band out of hot glue, you know that no matter what time it is, it's time to get crafty!

Supplies

Measuring tape

Watch face

Scissors

String

Glue gun of choice

Glitter glue sticks in any color

Silicone mat

Magnetic jewelry clasps

Instructions

1. Measure around your wrist, giving yourself a little space so the watch is not too tight.

2. Cut four lengths of string, each at least 3 inches longer than the length you measured. Thread each through the watch face around the bar for the band, as shown.

3. Use a dollop of glue at the point where each string attaches to keep the string and watch face in place on the silicone mat.

4. Tie each end of a magnetic jewelry clasp to one side of the watch band strings. Use your measuring tape to make sure that the distance between the two clasps is the total size you want the finished watch band to be.

5. Trim the extra string to about 2 inches in length or less.

6. Keeping the string tight by pulling on the clasp end, cover the string with glue, then fill in the watch band area with glue. Tuck the string ends into the glue of the watch band, and cover with glue.

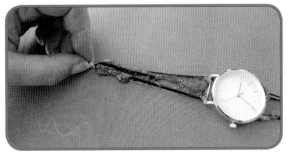

7. Repeat with the other side.

8. Allow to cool, but not to harden. Before the watch band hardens, shape it to your wrist. If you cannot keep the watch band around your wrist while the glue hardens, put it in a cup or place an object inside the band to keep the ends curved.

HACK: *If the band hardens before you can shape it properly, don't give up! You can use a heat gun to gently warm the glue again. This will soften the glue, giving you a second chance to shape your watch band.*

GLUE STICK EARRING HOLDER

At first glance this earring holder looks like an expensive glass jewelry stand—but it is actually made by fusing together mini glue sticks!

Supplies

14 mini glue sticks (plus glue in the glue gun)
Glue gun of choice

Silicone mat

Instructions

1. Place two glue sticks parallel to each other. Place two more glue sticks on top of the first two, log-cabin style. Glue the four corners in place.

2. Glue a fifth glue stick across the middle, parallel with the last two glue sticks. The glue stick pieces should resemble a ladder.

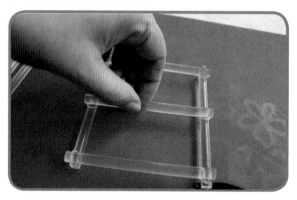

3. Repeat steps 1 and 2 to make a second piece that looks like a ladder.

4. Allow the ladder pieces to cool, then lean them against each other. Place two glue sticks on the bottom to measure the distance between the bottom ends.

5. Glue the two ladder pieces together at the top two joints. Allow to set, but not completely cool.

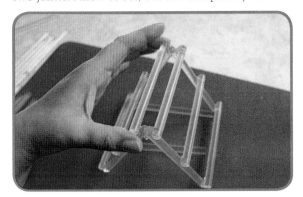

6. Set this piece on its side, then glue on the bottom two base pieces.

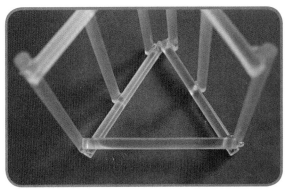

HACK: *Glue sticks don't have to be used in a glue gun to be useful! Consider using glue sticks in place of dowels or tongue depressors in craft projects.*

Entertaining and Parties

CORK AND GLUE COASTERS

With absorbent cork on the top and nonslip hot glue on the bottom, these coasters are fashionable, functional, and fun to make!

Supplies

Drinking glass

Pen

Roll of cork

Scissors

Glue gun of choice

Glue sticks of choice

Silicone mat

Instructions

1. Trace the drinking glass onto the back of the cork and cut out.

2. Fill the back of the cork with a layer of glue.

3. Carefully flip the coaster over and gently press flat onto the silicone mat.

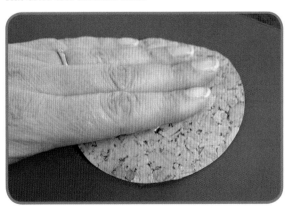

4. Allow to cool.

HEART CUPCAKE TOPPER

Gearing up for a party? Make some cupcake toppers with glue. Here we made heart-shaped toppers that would be great for Valentine's Day. You can, however, make these in any shape you would like to match your party theme. Break out the colored hot glue and a cookie cutter to get started!

Supplies

Cookie cutter in the shape of your choice

Silicone mat

Glue gun of choice

Colored glue sticks

Letter beads or embellishments (optional)

Toothpicks

Scissors

Instructions

1. Start by putting your cookie cutter on the silicone mat. Add glue along the inside edges, then continue to fill the cookie cutter with a thin pool of hot glue, working to the center. To minimize air gaps, be sure to squeeze the hot glue into each corner of the cookie cutter.

2. Once filled, you can add in letter beads or embellishments if desired while the glue is still warm. Otherwise, allow the piece to cool on the mat and in the cookie cutter.

3. Peel the project away from the mat once cool and carefully use your finger along the outside edge to free the topper from the cookie cutter.

4. You should be able to work it free easily. You can trim any rough edges with scissors for a cleaner look.

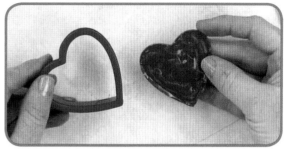

5. Turn the project over and add a bit of hot glue.

6. Add in a toothpick and allow to cool before topping your cupcakes.

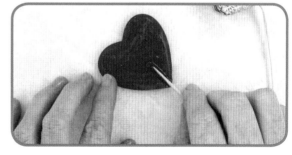

HACK: *A cookie cutter on a nonstick pad makes a great mold for hot glue!*

GLITTER SNOWFLAKES

These glitter snowflakes would be great added to a string for a party or even hanging on the Christmas tree. Make a bunch of them and add them to a winter wreath. However you use them, be sure to pick up enough glue to make several, as you will love how they turn out and how easy they are to make!

Supplies

Silicone mat

Glue gun of choice

White glitter, silver glitter, or metallic glue sticks

White glitter (optional)

Finger guards

Instructions

1. Search online for snowflake shapes. Print your favorite onto copy paper, then lay the silicone mat over the template.

2. Trace the lines of the template with glue and fill in any large areas with additional glue.

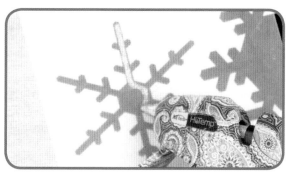

3. While still hot, liberally sprinkle glitter all over the project. This step is optional but creates a fun effect.

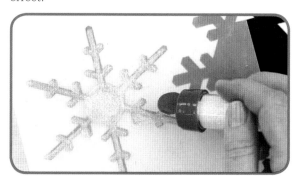

4. Use a finger guard and press glitter into snowflake while the project is still hot.

5. Allow the snowflakes to cool completely before peeling away from the mat. Use as is, or use additional glue to put the flakes on a string to make a banner.

HACK: *Once the glue gun is hot and the sticks are heated, remove any previous glue that is in your gun by squeezing onto the silicone mat. Once the glitter glue starts to come out you can continue with your project.*

CELEBRATORY CUPCAKE HOLDER

Add some sparkle to celebratory cupcakes with a glue cupcake holder. Make a single cupcake holder for a special occasion or make it a party with each cupcake in its own distinct holder!

Supplies

Cupcake holder template (page 126)
Silicone mat

Glue gun of choice
Glitter glue sticks

Instructions

1. Place the template under the silicone mat. Lines will be visible through a colored mat. Trace the bottom line with glue, then begin your design to fill in the template.

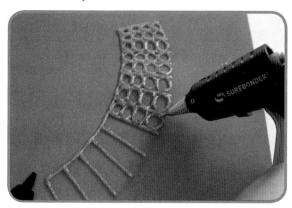

2. Allow the design to cool, then peel from the mat.

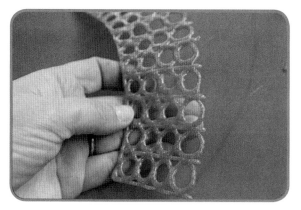

3. Wrap the ends together, then secure with glue. Hold in place until the glue sets.

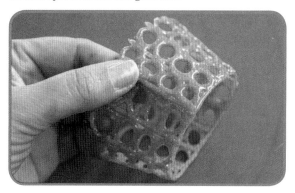

HACK: *Depending on the type of event, you can vary your design to suit the mood. An engagement party or anniversary might call for an organized design like the one shown here. For a cupcake holder that screams "wild and crazy," try a design inspired by the DIY Lampshade (page 35).*

SIMPLE NAPKIN RINGS

Add a crafty touch to your next holiday, dinner party, or simple dinner at home with the family by creating your own napkin rings.

Supplies

Glue gun of choice

Glue sticks of choice

Silicone mat

Measuring tape or ruler

Spray paint (optional)

Instructions

1. Draw a nickel-sized circle of glue onto the silicone mat.

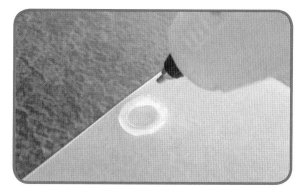

2. Add a second circle, then a third, overlapping the sides.

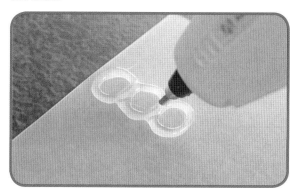

3. Keep adding circles in a straight line until it is 6 inches long. Allow to cool.

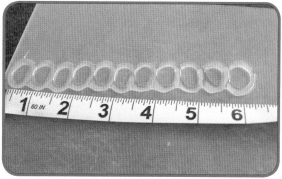

4. Peel up the cooled string of circles. Glue the two ends together to form the napkin ring. Hold in place until the glue sets.

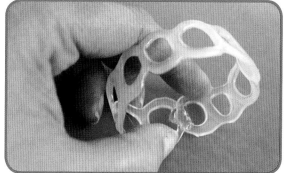

HACK: *Make a lot of napkin rings at once, then set them aside. Before a dinner party or special event, spray paint the napkin rings to match your decor. This way, you can always have custom napkin rings to match your party!*

PARTY CAKE TOPPER

Throwing a party and need to decorate the cake? This quick and easy cake topper can be made with just glue and some wood skewers. Glam up any cake with the word of your choice. From graduation parties to birthdays, this is a great craft idea to keep in your party crafting arsenal.

Supplies

Precision glue gun

Glitter or colored glue sticks

Pencil (optional)

Silicone mat

Wood skewers

Instructions

1. Start by planning out the word you want to use. You will need a "tail" on the letters at the beginning and end. Apply the glue directly to the silicone mat. Optionally, you can draw your word with pencil before adding glue.

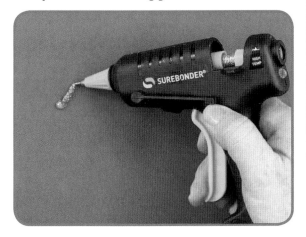

2. Continue until your entire word is complete, ending with a tail.

3. Wait for the glue to cool then lift just the tails from the silicone mat and glue to the wood skewers.

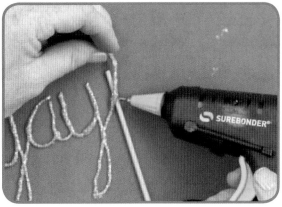

4. Go over the top of the word once more with an additional layer of colored glue.

5. Once complete, allow to cool and add to the top of your cake.

HACK: *For longer words, additional layers will be required for the word to stand up when lifted. You can flip over your project and use regular clear glue to add these layers if desired.*

MASON JAR FROG FOR FLOWER ARRANGING

A flower frog is an aid for arranging flowers. It helps them to stand up and look beautiful in a vase or, in this case, in a mason jar. Turn a mason jar lid into a flower frog with just a little glue and these instructions.

Supplies

Ring from a mason jar lid

Silicone mat

Glue gun of choice

Glue sticks

Instructions

1. Start by placing the jar ring on the silicone mat, then go around the inner edge with glue.

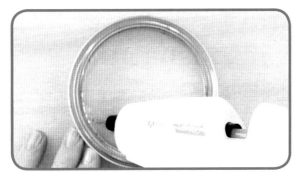

2. Add lines in one direction with the glue.

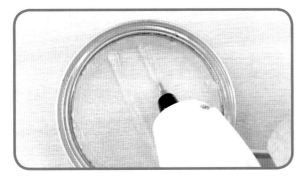

3. Add lines in the opposite directions with the glue.

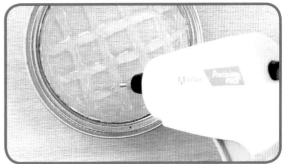

4. Allow the flower frog lid to cool completely on the mat.

5. Remove and add to the top of a mason jar and start adding flowers!

CUSTOM LETTERBOARD LETTERS

If you love letterboards but never have enough letters, this is your solution! Make your own letterboard letters out of glue to ensure you'll never run out of vowels! And as an added bonus, you can make your letters in fun colors or glitter!

Supplies

Flat toothpicks

Scissors

High-temp glue gun

Colored and glitter hot glue sticks

Silicone fondant molds in letter shapes

Felt letterboard

Heat gun (optional)

Instructions

1. From the wide end of the toothpick, cut a ½-inch piece. You will need one for each letter you make.

2. Using a very hot glue gun, fill the mold with hot glue. To minimize air gaps, be sure to squeeze glue into each corner of the mold. Before the glue sets, insert a cut toothpick piece into the base of the letter. Push all the way down, then pull up a little bit to keep the toothpick from showing through the front.

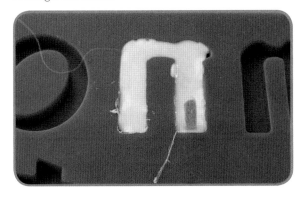

3. Repeat for all the letters. If you need more than one of any letter, wait until the letter cools, remove the piece, then make a second. Repeat as many times as needed.

4. Put the letters into the felt letterboard. If a toothpick is too long, trim it to the right length.

HACK: *You don't have to limit yourself to letters! Silicone fondant molds come in lots of fun designs—bows, seashells, nautical themes, and so much more!*

Crown template

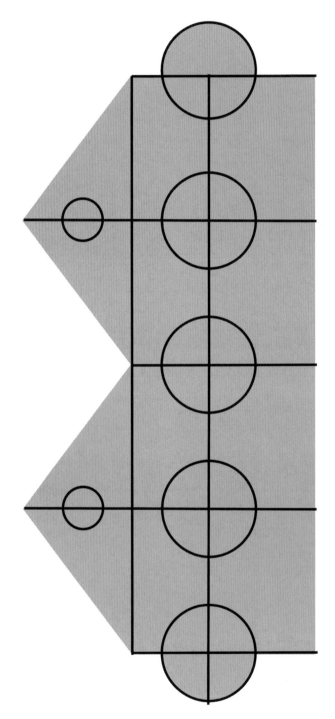

Christmas ornament templates

Cupcake holder template

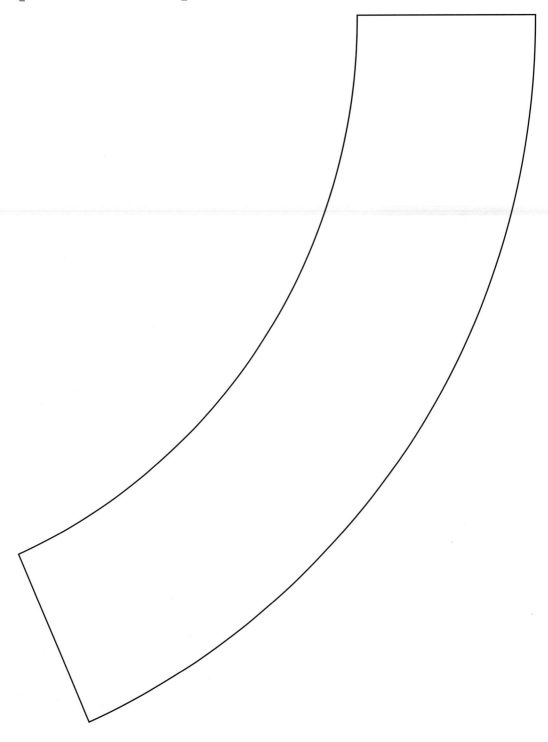

Hot Glue *Hacks and Crafts*

Acknowledgments

A special thanks to the following crafty friends who contributed projects to this book:

Carissa Bonham of CreativeGreenLiving.com

Once called "The Green Martha Stewart," Carissa lives near Portland, Oregon, with a house full of boys and a yard full of chickens. Carissa blogs at *Creative Green Living* about eco-friendly crafts and other sustainable projects including DIY, home decor, gardening, and chicken keeping—all from a nontoxic perspective.

Jen Goode of 100Directions.com

Jen Goode is a licensed artist, creative lifestyle blogger, and the Doodler in Charge at JGoode Designs, a Denver-based design studio. Her work has been featured in a number of publications, selling thousands of products. Jen is passionate about encouraging others to follow their own creative path.

Jessica Hill of MadInCrafts.com

Jessica Hill shares crazy good creativity on her blog *Mad in Crafts*. When she isn't crafting, she loves spending time with her family, watching the Detroit Tigers, and enjoying a local craft beer.

Gina Luker of TheShabbyCreekCottage.com

Gina Luker is the creative force behind the popular DIY blog *The Shabby Creek Cottage*, where she shares creative ways to eat, make, and decorate. She's a writer, photographer, and lover of all things aqua.

Kara Rodgerson of MineForTheMaking.com

Kara Rodgerson is a crafty lifestyle mom blogger behind *Mine for the Making*. She shares crafts, recipes, DIY projects, travel, and family fun on her blog. On any given day, you might find her multitasking in her office while snacking and jamming out to her favorite music of the month.

* * *

A special thanks to the following brands for supplying materials for the book: AdTech, Darice, DecoArt, Fiskars, Krylon, Plaid Enterprises, Surebonder, Testors, Westcott, and Wilton.

About the Authors

The hot glue gun was what drew **Angie Holden** to crafting from the start. She is the creative mind behind the popular craft blog *The Country Chic Cottage* (www.thecountrychiccottage.net) as well as a busy wife and mom of three. Angie blogs daily about creative crafts of all types and has worked with some of the top brands in the industry. When her glue gun is not plugged in, you might find her on the sidelines of a football game or relaxing on a farm in rural Tennessee.

Angie Holden and Carolina Moore

You'll never find **Carolina Moore** far from her glue gun. As a quick crafts guru and author of the website *30 Minute Crafts* (www.30MinuteCrafts.com), she spends her days creating original craft projects to share with her readers as well as working with some of the most popular craft brands in the industry. When she's not wielding her glue gun, you'll find her playing board games with her husband and their two young boys or teaching art in their classes. Carolina lives in San Diego, California.

In 2010, Angie and Carolina met online as craft bloggers. Though they live on opposite coasts, they first met in person in 2012 and see each other about twice a year for crafts-related events. They have cowritten websites together, been featured in YouTube videos, and cohost the bimonthly series Craft Lightning on their sites, sharing their love of fast crafts.